AEGEAN SUMMER

by
John L. Bowman

AEGEAN SUMMER

© 2012 John L. Bowman. All rights reserved.

No part of this book may be reproduced, stored in a retrieval system, or transmitted by any means without the written permission of the author.

ISBN: 978-0-692-99298-2

Any people depicted in stock imagery provided are models which are being used for illustrative purposes only.

This book was printed on acid-free paper.

Printed in the United States of America

Because of the dynamic nature of the Internet, any web addresses or links contained in this book may have changed since publication and may no longer be valid. The views expressed in this work are solely those of the author.

COVER

The cover is a picture of Mylopotas Bay on the island of Ios in the Aegean Sea in early summer of 1992. Ios is one of the Greek southern Cyclades Islands. The house I lived in is about fifth from the far end of the beach on the water— the one with all the trees. The water is as good as it looks. It is clean, warm, clear and calm. The beach is as white as it looks. The weather is also as good as it looks. It is an idyllic place. The inset is a picture of me taken in the fall of 1992, immediately after the summer.

TABLE OF CONTENTS
AEGEAN SUMMER

INTRODUCTION	1
CHAPTER ONE, BEFORE THE SUMMER My life before the summer	3
CHAPTER TWO, DURING THE SUMMER My life during the summer	15
CHAPTER THREE, AFTER THE SUMMER My life after the summer	43
CHAPTER FOUR, CONCLUSION Some final thoughts and observations on life and happiness	57
WORKS CITED	63

INTRODUCTION

This is a true story—it is about my journey to happiness in the summer of 1992. My friend George Macoubray read my story and decided to interrupt a successful career and do the same. In 2004, at age 42, George took time off from life to take his wife Marcy and two children to Europe. They spent three months traveling together as a family experiencing some of the best times of their lives. Tragically, within three years of their return, George's wife Marcy was diagnosed with cancer and died at age 47 on September 23, 2007. On her deathbed, Marcy asked to see the pictures of her family together on that trip and she said that journey was one of the most significant things she had done in her life. This was one of the last things she said. George and his family were devastated, but George had seized a snapshot of time in life to be happy that enriched his and his family's lives. We can all learn from George and Marcy's experience. Life is short—live it now before it is too late. This book is dedicated to the George and Marcy Macoubrays of this world who have the courage to live life now.

I believe anyone can do what they did and achieve happiness.

CHAPTER ONE

BEFORE THE SUMMER

It was like waking up from a nightmare and realizing that the life you are living is a nightmare. The alarm went off at 6:30 on an early morning in February 1992, and I was filled with the dread of another day at a job I hated. I lay there for a while hoping that my obligations for the day would just somehow disappear, but I knew that I had to get up and go through the same monotonous, pressure filled day I had for the last 20 years. I dragged myself out of bed, took a shower, put on the suit costume that symbolized my oppression and went to work.

I felt like shit because I had a hangover. I had gotten into the habit of drinking heavily after work because it was the only way to escape my depression from the daily obligations and grind. The headache, fatigue and heartburn were my morning companions now as I inched toward work in the morning freeway traffic. The cars on the road were filled with people with the same glassy, dazed stares the workers of America wear as they go to their jobs. I asked myself the same question I had asked every morning for the last 20 years, "Why am I doing this?" I thought the same thought I always thought, "There must be a better life…"

My life had become one of obligation and duty. Individually, these obligations were tolerable; collectively, they were overwhelming. I had so many roles it was almost confusing. I was a husband, father, son and employee. Each of these roles inexorably harnessed me to resentful obligations that stole my freedom. Above all, I had to be the breadwinner for my family, which indentured me into the role of a servile employee. I was giving away my life to these roles and obligations—I had lost my freedom. I could not do what I wanted to do. I felt trapped by society and circumstances—like I was in prison. As I drove, I played the same tape I always played—if Gauguin could leave his family and job in Paris to live in easy and cheap Tahiti, why can't I?

To make matters worse, this way of thinking made me an intolerable, miserable man to live with. I was angry, resentful and surly. Just look at me in a family photo when I am in my early thirties. Look at me—amongst the beauty of my wife and young daughters; I am a burning cauldron of self-destructive emotions. I felt like shit, I felt empty, life was monotonous, and I was deeply depressed. I was a thinking robot. I look angry, resentful, and surly because I was. My feelings colored all of my relationships, and I thought I was a misanthrope—I thought I did not like people, and the truth was I  really did not like people. I was someone who was what I was not. Tragically, my feelings contaminated my attitude toward my wife, children, and friends. I think this awful picture speaks a thousand words. I look like how I felt, and I look like a tyrant. I can hardly look at myself in this picture.

I was fortunate, perhaps driven, to marry for love. I was 23 years old and had just graduated from college. I went to a bar one evening with a friend, drank too much, and discovered two huge beautiful brown eyes looking at me across a smoke filled room. These were the same eyes as those of my mother, who used to look at me in my crib. The eyes were Kathy MaCoy's, and I was smitten. I did not know whether to introduce myself, kiss her, make love to her, or marry her—so

I did them all. We romanced, married, and started a family. She was a beauty from the small town of Newberg who was out on the town with her friends for her 21st birthday. She came from a solid family with the core American values of hard work and thrift. I did not know at the time, but she was also a kind, gentle, and virtuous woman. To my delight, she was also a sensual woman who enjoyed biology, like me. We just conjoined for the next forty years.

When I arrive at work, the artificial hype had already begun. Brokers rushing here and there like robots doing very important things. I had to shift to "on," there is no relaxing or idle speed here. Telephones ringing, faxes coming and going, computers spitting, huddled meetings, mail being delivered, and FedEx packages being sent were the shrill sounds of the morning. The brokers' sales meeting began at 7:30 and everyone, per the format, was expected to tell everyone else what they are doing and how successful they have been. Just beneath the artificial veneer of cooperation there is an icy mistrust in the air as everyone jockeys for position in the hierarchy of the group. The pressure has already begun at 7:30 a.m. and will not abate until the evening. The broker rankings have already come out for the month, so the pressure is on those at the bottom to produce. Their embarrassment and fear of losing their jobs is palpable. The management has done a good job of creating an air of fear and competition among the combatants. The stage has been set that pits each person against everyone else.

I was in an artificial environment filled with artificial people. It was all one big strange hierarchy of machines where machines existed within machines. At the bottom were the faxes and the ubiquitous, rude and demanding telephones. At the top was the overarching contrived company machine controlling and directing all the other machines—the master machine, integrated, interdependent, and closely meshed. Squeezed in the middle were the human machines. We human machines were all like the machines that rang and spat and did what we were programmed to do. We were just part of a bigger artificial machine. I was just one of those machines, like the fax machines, with no separate essence. I had no inherent value as a human being; rather, my value was measured on how well I integrated with the machine. I was just a gear. All the people were machines, and they all were artificially, like me, playing their part in the machine. This is no *deus ex machina*, but rather a mindless machine cranking out depressingly servile roles to play. Using machines, being a machine, and being part of a bigger machine did not bring me peace or happiness. It was a contrived environment filled with many masters and demands, unconcerned with my humanness or happiness.

After the meeting, I walk fast to my cubicle. Everyone walks fast because they need to look busy and important. There is no time to relax. My cubicle is a 7´ x 7´ enclosure with 6´ walls where I spend 50% of my life. I sit down and feel claustrophobic and trapped. It is a prison without privacy. It is like living life in a cell. It is surrounded by other cubicles with brokers making calls and deals. The cubicles are designed in such a way so you can hear other brokers making deals, which causes everyone to fear falling behind, so a kind of feverish competition is created with each trying to outdo the other. It is like controlled panic. This goes on all day, and there is no peace.

I, like many working fathers today, was utterly oblivious to the significance of my children. I was so preoccupied with myself that I failed to appreciate my offspring, who were parts of me, my being, and my future. I failed to understand that my relationship with them is one of the closest and enduring relationships to be had. I had little time for my children. I did not spend the time to enjoy their developing personalities, natural affection, and playfulness. I was too busy. I did not grasp the fleeting moment of their youth; a special time in any parent's life that goes as quickly as it came. I did not know how rich a man I was to have these three young beings in my life. Maude "the rebel" was 11, Abbey "the sensitive one" was 7, and Sydney "the formidable one" was 2. What a damn fool I was.

Then the phone starts ringing: clients demanding to know why a listing has not moved, other brokers requesting information, prospects calling, problems in deals and difficult buyers and sellers making demands. Here I was at 9:00 in the morning hyped up, pressured, dealing with a multitude of other people's problems with a hangover and resentment over having to even be there. I feel like a small cog in a huge, impersonal machine. I was unimportant, insignificant and boxed in. My speed is regulated by someone else—I must speed up when they pull the accelerator and slow down when they hit the brakes. My speed is entirely determined by someone else. I had no control over my existence—I had lost my free will. I thought to myself, I could be on some beach in Cozumel just waking up to the sound of the tropical sea and a balmy breeze, relaxed, free and happy. I knew I actually could be there but could not bring myself to do it because I feared losing my job, my income, and my home. My life was been relegated to handling the affairs of others instead of doing the things I really wanted to do like travel, think philosophy, learn, or write.

I had been working in the commercial real estate business for ten years, and my depression had been an evolving experience. We all have bosses, but one of my bosses was an angry man who made my life miserable. He had a volatile temper, he was quick to anger, he had a fearful delivery and he used his anger to control people—including me. I was young at the time, and I lived in constant fear of him at the office. It was like walking on eggshells; he could explode capriciously at any moment for any reason. Meetings were particularly harrowing because I knew if I said the wrong thing he would instantly blow up, striking fear in everyone's heart. I felt awful, unconfident, I was humiliated, I felt degraded, and I was on the verge of losing my self-respect. I was living a brutish life at the hands of a brutish person. In hindsight, I think the American workplace with its demands for production, pressures on managers to perform, and competitive environments engender this kind of person who totally disregards individual dignity and happiness. I think I was just one of many American workers facing capricious power.

This work experience humiliated me—and I defended myself in a predictable way. When people are threatened with anger, they get angry themselves. I learned that the best way to deflect my boss's anger was with anger. I discovered that my boss was fearful of others' anger, so I also got angry. Anger became my shield, my protector and my sword. But this solution had only short-term benefits and a long-term downside—once I learned anger, I also learned how to use it to control others. I began using anger in my relationships, including my family, so they became angry and resentful in return, and the result was an awful downward spiral in my life of living with angry people. As they say, shit runs downhill. It was awful, and I became more depressed as my relationships deteriorated and sought escape in alcohol. It was a lethal brew: anger, humiliation, self-destruction, and alcohol. This cycle of experience scared me for years and was only healed during my Aegean summer.

Here is a picture taken of me at work when I was in my early thirties. I am in a sales meeting and look like mindless machine-like employee. This photo speaks to me. I see all my feelings at that time. I am depressed, angry, and humiliated, seeking escape in my work. I had to focus on my work because I had a family to support, which made me resentful because it was for them I had to endure this hell. In this picture, I am figuring out how to make money and beat my competition. I was good at both, but I was deeply unhappy.

This is a special day that I dread because I have a sales evaluation meeting with the sales manager. The purpose of the meeting is to determine how much I am producing under the guise of helping me succeed. In reality it is management gathering information on me in order to determine if I stay or go. The atmosphere is cordial but serious, and I spend considerable time explaining what I am doing in order to justify my job. I am a disposal pawn that is of value only to the extent that I add value to the game. I am judged by another, and they determine my worth. My boss's judgment becomes my prison. I emerge from the meeting with fear, angst, and a tremendous feeling of pressure to succeed and produce. I have been mentally set up in a viscous competition that does not cease.

I think competition between human beings is natural, but American business enterprises, in order to succeed, often contrive inter-company rivalry and competition—and the American worker is the victim. Let me explain why I think this with two hypothetical farmers. Farmer A competes against farmer B to raise more crops, and the one who raises the most makes more money. The competition between these imaginary primitive farmers involves real issues like the weather, the condition of their soil, ingenuity in crop rotation, planting times, and effort. This is natural competition. But farmer A artificially alters the game in order to best farmer B. He has four sons, to each of which he allocates one quarter of his farm. He tells them that their success does not ride on besting farmer B, but rather on besting each other. The resulting internecine competition between the brothers is artificial because one person owns the whole farm of which they are a part. When farmer A induces completion between his sons, he sets the parts against the whole, which causes each son to advance his own interests and not that of the whole. The result is a kind of artificial completion that may best farmer B, but sows distrust and rivalry between the brothers, and similarly the employees of today. Only farmer A emerges the winner. This is artificial competition. I was one of those "brothers" living in the same fog of contrived ignorance. This old contrived game has been magnified today, and the victims are many American workers.

The entire afternoon is spent forcing myself to do what I do not want to do. I must make calls, I must deal with problems, I must get listings, and I must beat my competition. I push myself even though I feel terrible and tired. All I really want is to find some place of peace and sleep. Around mid-afternoon my body would say, take a rest. It would say, I need to take a nap. My eyes were half closed, my mind was slow, and my body was fatigued. My whole being was screaming for rest. But my obligations pushed me on, and I struggled my way through my fatigue. My body was completely divorced from nature—from natural time and the rhythms of biology.

Jeremy Rifkin in his book *Time Wars* explained how our conception of time has evolved from the natural cycles of nature to measurable hours, minutes, seconds, and now, with the computer, nanoseconds. It seems as industrial societies become more complex they require punctuality and cooperation, which requires an artificial kind of time that synchronizes our efforts. My job was a manifestation of this new kind of time. I had to be at a place at an exact time, I had to make reports by a certain time, and I was expected to start and stop working at preordained times. These time-events had nothing to do with my psyche, my body or my happiness. They were just incessant demands on my short time to live. For me, time became an obstacle to either endure or outpace. I mostly endured it, but I also was swept up with the mob trying to get ahead of the clock. The more successful I became in time-management, the more people I could talk to and the more deals I could juggle, which allowed me to be more productive and make more money. I was obsessed with time and speed. But human-time was becoming my enemy because I knew it was ruining my life. My life under nanoseconds had become breathless and sterile. It allocated no time for me to enjoy what nature offers. I just had to get out Dante's hell.

After work, I face the same traffic jam and frustration getting home—tired, exhausted and spent. I wasted a day of my short time here on Earth. I thought to myself that I was just part of a herd—I went to work with the herd and am now going home with the herd. I am crowded together mindlessly following the herd to someplace I know not where. I just exist. As an individual, I am invisible—I am just one cow in a heard who goes to work every day and does the same damn thing day after day, month after month, and year after year. For me, the end of life was death.

Sigmund Freud in his *Civilization and its Discontents* said that we are constitutionally unable to avoid suffering and achieve true happiness. He wrote that because we are faced with the powerful exigencies of nature, feeble bodies, and the inability to adjust to relationships with others, states, and societies, we are doomed to live unhappy lives. For Freud, the only way I could increase my pleasure and happiness and decrease my suffering was chemically through drugs such as alcohol. This is precisely what I did. But, as Freud explained, with chemicals I was not seeking happiness but rather quietness. I was seeking to numb my pain. In my daydreams, I began imagining alternate worlds in order to break off all relations with reality. I would imagine myself as Gauguin living in Tahiti, or myself free and happy in a world where I had not taken on the responsibilities of family. But the problem, as Freud pointed out, is that I achieved nothing with these illusions because reality is too strong. So, at age 42, it seemed I had arrived at Freud's place of inexorable unhappiness.

Unhappiness is an awful disease. It colored and warped my whole life. I was supremely unhappy. William James once wrote,

> The attitude of unhappiness is not only painful, it is mean and ugly. What can be more base and unworthy than the pining, puling, mumping mood, no mater by what outward ills it my have engendered? What is more injurious to others? What less helpful as a way out of difficulty? It but fastens and perpetuates the trouble which occasioned it, and increases the total evil of the situation. (James 89)

I was at the bottom—a place bereft of hope for a better life. I was in a very black place.

And then one gray and rainy morning I changed. It was a morning so typical of Oregon and my mental state. I was lying in bed after having been awakened by the dreaded clock of doom, depressed, staring at the ceiling and feeling like I just could not face another day. It was in this comatose state that I was struck with a thought that changed my life. It occurred to me that my life was half over and, unless I did something, the last half of my life would simply be more of the same. I was seized by the thought that time is rapidly running out and that I must act now if anything was going to change. I thought to myself, "What have I got to lose?" If I do nothing I will be unhappy for the rest of my life, but if I change things my life just might get better. It was like having a religious epiphany. It was at this juncture that my mind just went another direction. I realized that I was really free, like a free animal in the wild, and not as a trapped one in a zoo, and that my circumstances were of my own making. It struck me that if I had made these circumstances, I could damn well change them. I thought to myself that I am in truth free. I resolved then and there to change my life. My emotional reaction was electric. I got an instant rush of elation, happiness and liberation. I was swept with a feeling of relief. It was like being saved from a firing squad at the last second. My burdens just seem to evaporate, and my demons went to look for other victims. Necessity knows no laws. I decided to throw my remaining fate to the winds of fortune.

 It has been said in order to survive in a storm a ship should seek the open sea. On the open sea, it is untethered and thus freed to rely on its own ability to ride the waves. If it stays in harbor close to land, it will get smashed upon the shoreline. When we face times of trouble, we must look to ourselves for support and guidance. We should trust our own instincts and rhythms to determine what's right for us. The shoreline of convention will smash us to bits if we stay too close. I went to sea.

 I said that watershed morning to my wife lying next to me, "Kath, let's drop out," she said, "Okay" and within five minutes of excited brainstorming we had a plan. I sprang into action. I went straight to the office that morning and told my boss I was taking a sabbatical. It really did not matter what he said because I was thinking I may not return. I then listed my house for sale. I was lucky because numerous buyers wanted it, and I was able to make a quick sale for all cash. I took the sales proceeds and paid off all of my debts and put what was left over in the bank. I also used some of the proceeds to pay for travel expenses. I then rented a mini storage warehouse and moved all of my belongings into it when the sale closed. Within two months of my epiphany, I quit my job, was homeless, had shed most of my responsibilities, sold or stored all of my possessions, and become debt free. I was a happy man. I was exhilarated with the sense of freedom and prospect of adventure. My attitude was that I was going to see what fortune brought me. I was prepared to sever all ties with my past life, strike out on life anew, and never return. It is daunting to leave the security of a settled life—but I was prepared to do just that. I had transcended my comfort zone and lost my need for certainty in the future. Everything was new and exciting.

    I had spent most of my life seeking security. I had always focused on making money, paying bills, and saving for my daughters' college education and retirement. I had always lived in the future, doing what I had to do today to provide for a secure tomorrow. But with this philosophy of life, I had lost all spontaneity. I had left no room for joy, adventure or happiness. I had built my own prison, and if I was to escape it, I needed courage to risk my security for the possibility of a better life. There were no guarantees that my life would get better—indeed, my life could get much worse. The prospect of poverty was particularly fearful, but I had spent a good part of my life driven by this fear, and it was time to overcome it. I had to find the courage to accept risk, and I did.

    The winds of fate were warm. It is funny how things serendipitously happen when you have a goal. The wind truly works, and the world truly does stand aside for the man with a goal. When my mother and step-father heard of our plans, they got excited and wanted to come along. They knew of a house in on the island of Ios in Greece that we could rent. My employer gave me a sabbatical, and many people, including my clients, were understanding and encouraging. Many even took to living vicariously through my adventure. Even my dog found a place to stay.

Suffering is a ubiquitous human condition—so what else is new? The question is not whether you can endure your suffering, but rather what do you do about it. You have two choices as I see it—act or be acted upon. I had decided to act.

Kathy and I were 40 and 42 years old, respectively, when we boarded a plane with our children headed for London, England one early morning in early June 1992. Here we are at Portland International Airport, stroller and all. My life of pain was behind me and my uncertain life of adventure laid ahead. I cannot describe the exhilaration I was feeling.

CHAPTER TWO

DURING THE SUMMER

In hindsight, I am amazed at how quickly my previous life evaporated. I was so preoccupied with my exciting present that my nightmarish past quickly became just a bad dream. I was awake and filled with excitement, optimism, and the prospect of a grand and exciting adventure. We first flew to London and then Athens. We spent some time in Athens adjusting to Greek life and then boarded a ferry for our destination, the island of Ios. Ios is an island in the southern Greek Cyclades Islands located north of Santorini. It was to be our home for the next three months.

We docked at the city of Hora, which is a sea of white houses, on a bright sunny day and immediately drove over a large hill to our new home. At the crest of the hill, we paused to absorb the view—a view that is on the cover of this book. My spirits soared when I saw Mylopotas

Bay for the first time. It was picture perfect—a large lagoon of pristine, azure water with a white crescent sandy beach. We had made arrangements to rent a Greek house on the bay from an American family. We drove the length of the waterfront to the house entrance, which was just a few steps from the water. The first thing we did was put on our bathing suits and go swimming. My Aegean summer began, and it was to be the experience of my lifetime.

The house was a typical white Greek home with blue shutters and a large patio in front that overlooked the water. The home was an oasis. The house was in the middle of a jungle of plants and trees bounded by a rock fence. There was a grand entrance to the house through a rock pathway surrounded by lush greenery. At one end was the sandy beach and the water, and at the other was the patio facing the water. The house itself was stucco construction, single story with trellised patios in back and on the side. It was U-shaped with a kitchen and living room just off the front patio. There was a partially enclosed courtyard at back. The courtyard was surrounded by bedrooms and a bathroom. Throughout the house were large swinging double doors and windows that, when opened, brought the garden into the house. It was like living in a garden with a steady fresh warm ocean breeze flowing throughout all living spaces. Behind the house were the barren rock strewn hills of the island, a contrast that accentuated the house's luxuriant compound. It was a place of refuge that invited total relaxation. It was a place apart from the world. It was all that I could want.

The weather was perfect. It had a dry tropical feel. It was warm but not hot. It was comfortable and not sultry. The steady breeze wafting from the bay constantly rustled the trees and palms. Above all, it was the water. The house faced a white sandy beach that gently sloped down to low waves and the bay. The water was clean, crystal clear and warm. It was water made for swimming and playing. I was totally absorbed into a place and setting that satisfied all of my wildest dreams of what a utopia away from work would be like. It was perfect.

I quickly settled into a daily routine, which was to get up late in the morning after a long and restful sleep and have my coffee on the veranda overlooking the bay in a state of total peace. I learned that long and deep sleep is an essential ingredient for happiness. It made me rested, relaxed, and serene. After breakfast I would walk the path to the white sandy beach and go swimming in the warm, crystal clear Aegean Sea. The rest of the morning I would sit on the veranda and read.

In the afternoon I would often continue my reading, take some family excursion into town, hike along the beach, go shopping for groceries, or just spend the afternoon on the beach playing and swimming with the family. My children loved the beach. I also ran most afternoons for exercise. I found that the more I relaxed the more I enjoyed exercise. I ran and swam and ran and swam. I lost weight, became extremely fit and felt strong. I could feel my blood pressure going down and my body relaxing. The knot in my stomach completely disappeared. All of the artificial characteristics I had acquired in order to succeed in business evaporated. I became less aggressive, less competitive, and less suspicious.

In the warm evenings the family would have dinner together either in the dining room or on one of the verandas. Dinnertime was a period of bustling, cooking, eating, chatting, laughing, and dishwashing. The dinners were filled with family chatter and laughter. After dinner we would all move to the rooftop veranda to watch the sun go down. These evenings were magical. They encompassed an environment of family love and togetherness accentuated by mild inebriation, a beautiful and serene sunset over the bay, the sound of the water, and a warm tropical breeze as dusk descended. After the family went to bed, my step-father Curt and I would stay up and drink Metaxa 5 Star Brandy and discuss our day's readings.

Curt was a delightful intellectual with a broad liberal arts education. He was a kind and learned person whose character embodied many of the characteristics of my ideal father figure. He came from a distinguished Oregon family and had spent most of his life in the United States Diplomatic Corps in Africa. He was urbane, sophisticated, and very liberal. He liked to call himself politically a "New Deal Roosevelt Democrat." He was a mild and thoughtful man. He had retired from government service and moved back to Portland, where he had grown up. He met my mother in his late sixties, had a whirlwind romance and  they married. Curt and I became intellectual soul mates. We would debate the character of Cervantes's Don Quixote, examine the merits of Mill's utilitarianism, weigh Gibbons's reasons for the decline of the Roman Empire, and discuss the relative merits of Stravinsky's dissonant *Firebird Suite*. Our talks ranged, and I was filled with an intense interest in everything.

Curt and my discussions went on for hours and became increasingly profound as the summer progressed. We plumbed many of the fascinating depths of the human experience. We talked about the meaning of life, the fear of death, the nature of desire, and what constitutes happiness. The more we drank the smarter we became, and the more we congratulated each other on our keen insight and ability to solve all the world's problems. We debated and laughed a lot. My intellectual curiosity was challenged and fulfilled. I was talking about and thinking about the things I never used to have the time for. I was living in a way that fulfilled every need my body and psyche demanded for happiness.

M. M. Kirsch in his book *How to Get Off the Fast Track and Live a Life Money Can't Buy* said that the happy life consists in raising one's aspirations beyond materialism. Happiness and fulfillment come from:

> Living a life of simplicity that [allows] the individual time to wonder and appreciate the simple joys in life. To live the good life [is] to be able to control one's life and one's destiny, and not be at the mercy of the marketplace.

I was taking the time to wonder and appreciate the simple joys of life away from the demands of business. I had taken control of my life, and I was no longer a slave to the office. I found myself, as Kirsch said, appreciating what I had rather than striving for more. I was being myself, and I was devoting more energy to the really important aspects of my life. I was just living more simply. It began dawning on me that these ideas are the true prescriptions for happiness.

My mother was a wonderfully difficult character. She could be best described as a very lively "Auntie Mame" who thought the worst of all sins was to be boring.

She never told me to be moral, diligent, or conscientious—rather only never to be boring. She lived up to her maxim and lived every day of her life like it was her last. She loved parties, people, and her children. She loved men, married three times, and had innumerable beaus. She could also be a real pain in the ass. She loved to stir up trouble just so she could announce a new crisis was at hand. She loved crises. She would come alive when contention was brewing and relished stirring the pot. What I did come to appreciate was the added sense of family my mother and Curt brought to my Aegean experience. It occurred to me that most American families consist of only one or two generations—adults alone together or parents with children. The essence of a family is enhanced with the presence of many generations; the vanguard avuncularly observing and helping, the working middle generation shouldering the responsibilities, and the new generation, all with biological and traditional family ties. I had been given the rare opportunity to have the time to immerse myself into the rich tapestry of family.

Bertrand Russell said in *The Conquest of Happiness* that family is one of the greatest sources of happiness and, conversely, one of the greatest sources of unhappiness today because it has become so derailed and disorganized. He believed parenthood has the potential of offering the greatest and most enduring happiness life has to offer. With children, we are not an isolated individual but rather part of a stream of life flowing from some original germ to some unknown future. Those without children isolate themselves from this stream. For parents, the future is important because their children are part of it, and for grandparents, children are important because they revive their past and represent their legacy. My Aegean summer allowed me to recognize and experience that stream of life, which was an experience I was too busy to appreciate when I was at the office all day.

Unbeknownst to me, my wife was the wind beneath my wings. I did not know it at the time, but I was very lucky that I had found this woman to marry—and that she had consented to do so. She was everything I needed—moral, solid, prudential and even-tempered. I learned that I had taken her for granted. I had the time to notice her irreplaceable significance in managing our family affairs. She cared for our children, cared for me, and was the glue that kept the family together. She was also intrepid and willing to cast her fate with me on this unknown adventure. I watched as she navigated the difficulties of living on Ios. She endured having to wash clothes in the bathtub, cooking with antiquated appliances and bugs. One of the first nights on Ios Kathy woke up to her worst nightmare—an army of creeping large and small noisy bugs on the netting that covered everyone's bed. From that point on she slept little and kept a nightly vigil with two shoes warding off the bugs.

In spite of the challenges, Kathy had fun. One of her first experiences with Greek culture was in Athens when some men in a tavern, spotting her with her three small children, said, "You are a rich woman." The Greeks love children. She was accepted by the Greek women at the local grocery store as one of their own. One elderly woman asked her to get her water, a gesture that meant she was like her daughter. She became the de facto interpreter of English for the Greeks at the local grocery store. The Greeks took to her: the owner of Far Out, a local tavern, gave her rides, Demetri the groundskeeper gave her advice on how to cook Greek style, and one amorous Greek asked her for a date. She said she was married, and he responded with "so what?" Many of the women on the beach would go topless, which was not part of my wife's repertoire—for long. By the end of the summer I found her on the sand soaking up the sun topless. The truth is I was fortunate to have a soulmate who  was as open to change and willing to explore alternative futures as I was. In many ways, she enabled my Aegean summer.

My relationship with my wife improved dramatically. We were no longer burdened by overwhelming outside demands. The ease of life allowed us to reconnect as friends. She looked great, and we made more time for lovemaking. It was much better than the books. I came to remember why I fell in love with her. I loved her beauty, and I was reminded of her wonderful optimistic and happy personality, as well as her caring nature. I fell in love again with the woman with whom I had once fallen in love. I realized I had come to assume she would always be there to do her duty to me and the children. It occurred to me that for many successful men, their marriages just die like an untended garden. Their appreciation and love for the woman they chose fades with time due to neglect. I was lucky to recognize this at 42 years old and recapture the love with the love of my life.

Bertrand Russell wrote that much happiness comes from affection. Those who feel themselves unloved sink into timid despair and become self-centered and insecure. They become introverted and melancholy. Looking outward and valuing others for their intrinsic qualities, like your spouse, is the antidote. Valuing others turns you away from yourself and allows you to focus on others. In my case, the other was one who loved me, my wife, and the rekindled feeling of love was electric. Russell said that the capacity for genuine affection for another is one mark of the man who has escaped from the isolated and barren prison of self. Kathy was my life companion, and I came to re-appreciate both her and the importance of having someone significant to go through life with together. I was finally escaping from my prison of self.

When I was working, I focused so much of my time and energy on business and making money that I also failed to appreciate another joy that had always been just under my nose. My children were little, rambunctious, and yeaning for love and affection. I gave it, but lurking behind my giving was a deep resentment for having incurred the obligation to raise and support children. It was a feeling that manifested itself in innumerable unknown ways that I know my children sensed. I would imagine how free I could have been in life without these black holes of responsibility. In hindsight, I believe I was so focused on myself, business and money that I failed to appreciate the utter wonder of creating new human beings from my own body. I realized that I had been missing the opportunity to watch these nascent beings flourish into a human that contained much of me, which is a rare and rewarding experience for a parent. I began to ask myself thought-provoking questions like what my life would have been like if I never had children. I asked myself whether there were more meaningful things that I could have done with my life—and if so, what they would be. Perhaps I could have made more money, gained more prestige or power, or have enjoyed more sensual pleasure. But then I asked myself: Once I had done these, then what? I think many American businessmen unthinkingly pursue these false gods and find themselves fifty or sixty years old, empty, seeking new pleasures and unhappy. It occurred to me that in our competitive society, many American men fail to appreciate their children in their lifetimes. Many divorce, move on in life, lose touch with their children, and tragically never know what they had lost. I was lucky, I learned during my Aegean summer to appreciate what I had.

I have three daughters. Maude was eleven and on the cusp of entering the tunnel. I believe that parents' influence on their children ends in their early teens when they enter a tunnel. In the tunnel they learn the ways of their peers, develop their own personalities independent of their parents, and gradually mature. I think that children then emerge at the other end of the tunnel at various times, but usually in their early twenties. I was fortunate to experience a bit of Maude's pre-tunnel person. She had an independent spirit,  élan for life, single-mindedness, and desire to learn. During the summer, she read Homer's *Iliad*, which was quite a feat for an eleven year old.

Abbey was seven and deep into childhood. Abbey was a sensitive and kind child. I knew this, but I had never had the time to appreciate her other qualities, like her sense of humor. She was funny. Mother was getting somewhat of a stomach in her older age, and one day Abbey put a pillow in her shorts and mimicked mom. We all laughed at the spontaneous spoof, but I think mom laughed the hardest.

Sydney, like many two year olds, had a happy and joyful personality. She was interested in everything that was going on. She was utterly spontaneous with

affection and touch. I had forgotten about the significance of touch with my children. Children are innocent, sensual creatures who innately want lots of skin. I loved the skin, it was intimate and heart-warming. Perhaps it was these early traits that allowed Sydney to grow into the incredible, self-confident, relentless, and formidable woman she is today.

My Aegean summer gave me the chance to enjoy my young daughters and their forming personalities before they became adults. It allowed me to change my attitude from one that saw them as black holes of obligation to, well, my children—my progeny. They touched my heart. I came to be amazed that my wife and I had created such beauty. I think it was a beauty I would never have seen, like many American businessmen, had I not made the effort to change my life.

Greek culture is much slower than American culture. It is a lifestyle that is easier and more human oriented. I suppose I could have taken my sabbatical in places like France, Mexico, or Hawaii, but it would not have been the same. There was something special about Greece—it was a fortuitous choice. Many consider Greece the crucible of Western civilization. Before Alexander the Great's conquest of Persia in the late third century BCE, Greece consisted of political entities called a *polis*—or small close-knit communities consisting of families and extended relatives. These *polises* valued human bonds like father-child, mother-child, and cousin-cousin over many of the artificial bonds created by commerce, and destroyed bonds caused by divorce, that we find in America today. Our emphasis on money, competition, success and prestige are interfering with these primitive human associations that the ancient Greeks so valued. It seems to me that American culture has subordinated familial relations to mammon. Because of this I had lost my bearings, which Greek culture allowed me to reacquire. Greece also has a history of being close to the land, a tradition America once had until its industrialization. Many Americans like me live in urbanized environments that are separated from agriculture and nature. We have little understanding of the slow comforting patterns of nature like the magic of dusk and dawn, the sound of water or just the awesome silence of nature. The agricultural orientation of Ios brought me closer to nature, and I found myself more allied with nature rather than opposed to it. Our house, for example, was amidst a garden, and not roads and malls, and the sounds were of waves and braying donkeys, not cars. My summer in Greece enabled me to experience a more nature-oriented human culture.

Nobel Prize winning Egyptian writer Nagib Mahfouz wrote on Western culture's influence on traditional Egyptian society, or cultures like Greece. He described ancient times, when friends met and took time off to socialize and reconnect. Human contact was more important than time and money to traditional Egyptians. He wrote how Western culture changed this. With our mantra that time is money, our relationships become judged on some ubiquitous monetary scale. We come to think how much of our precious time this person is taking—time that could be employed gainfully to make more money. From my experience in Greece and my reading of Mahfouz, I learned that much of my life had been artificial—it was a time- and money-oriented existence that had been created by other people. My office had consisted of clocks measuring when to work, cubicles designating where to work, and labels like clients and sales managers identifying for whom to work. It was not real—it was a human-created hell for the sake of productivity. I

began to understand that I did not need this kind of societal and commercial chimera to be happy.

I began to experience the synthetic layers of characteristics I had acquired in order to be successful in business slowly peel away, like layers of an onion. One of the most significant onion-skin characteristic I began to shed was the ever-present feeling of competition. In my office, I always feared falling behind my competitors. It was an awful feeling because my sense of self-worth was at stake. On Ios, there were no competitors—the people were simpler. Our groundskeeper Demetri's simplicity was refreshing. He invited us to his house and served us Coca Cola as we sat on his bed with a television soap opera on in the background for entertainment. He wanted to know if he could visit us in Oregon while he was in Kentucky seeing his brother, unaware that Oregon and Kentucky are 3,000 miles apart. There were no clocks to measure time, no computers to interpret reality, and no cell phones to keep me in instantaneous touch with the world. There was no television, that ubiquitous window to the world, in our home. Much to my wife's chagrin, there also were no washing machines, dryers or hot water. It was all natural, and I became more natural. I learned that there is nothing wrong with doing nothing—you just have to relax into it. I also learned that self-worth does not come from contrived circumstances that require you to best your contemporaries. My life has an intrinsic value that transcends others' ideas of what constitutes human worth.

During my years in commercial real estate, I always felt a nagging loss of something, and I could never quite put my finger on what it was. I felt my life was limited, going nowhere, and narrow. I always felt a need to see more, do more, and most significantly, know more. I was always so tired, and my mind was always so preoccupied with deals, money and competition that I had little time to think of other things, like ideas. I just had no time alone to think. I was fortunate in that I had received a good liberal arts education at Whitman College when I was young, and I think it was this that was the kindling that drove me to want to know more about the human condition, and in particular the nature of happiness. It was no surprise then that I immersed myself in books and reading during my summer on Ios. I read in the morning when I got up, I read in the afternoon and I read late into the evening. I had set a goal of reading the *Norton Anthology of World Masterpieces* and the *Masterpieces of World Philosophy*. I read them both, which  made my summer more a mental journey than a physical one. The reading was so interesting, intense, and expansive that I got to the point where I could not wait to read. It was almost better than sex.

I want to describe some of the ideas I was exposed to during my summer because I think they demonstrate the limits to our thinking, indeed our lives, under the influence of a commercial culture. I think knowing these ideas frees us from our societal chains, which enables us to rewrite our beliefs in a way that offers the potential for happiness.

I read some of the very best literature and philosophy humankind has written throughout human history, and it was exhilarating. I read everything from the prehistoric *Epic of Gilgamesh* and the Old Testament to Aleksandr Solzhenitsyn's *Matryona's Home* and Doris Lessing's *The Old Chief Mshlanga*. I read Thoreau, who wrote about dancing to a different drummer, unnecessary worries, competition and getting ahead, and those who live lives of quiet desperation. Erasmus wrote about the joy of ignorance, Tolstoy on the value of life, and Sartre on the existentialist void and the need to be moral in an evil world. I was thrilled with Cervantes's words on courage, ideals and romance, Hobbes social contract and Swift's engaging and humorous account of human nature and our limitations. Boethius's *Consolation of Philosophy* and the wheel of fortune was one of my favorites. Once we put our fate in circumstances beyond our control, we lose happiness.

There is just so much to know, so much that ought to be known, and so little time to learn it. In commerce I had little time for ideas because I did not have time for ideas that did not relate to making money. I think of knowledge as a timeless river that few humans touch. This river extends back thousands of years and forward into the unknown future flowing with ideas, theories, and perceptions—an ever-changing body of knowledge. The river consists of all the great thoughts the best human thinkers have thought—it is a metaphoric collective river of the best ideas humankind has to offer. It is a cumulative river where new ideas are built on old ideas and the result is an ever-increasing river of better ideas. Some swim in this river and others do not. Most humans are too busy, too lazy or just not interested in this river. I was, and I had the opportunity to explore, indeed participate, in that river during my Aegean summer.

Alexander Pope's *Essay on Man* reminded me that we are a small part of a whole, or part of an unchanging and timeless *Chain of Being*, and that it is only our pride that causes us to think we are the center of the universe. Montaigne is a wonderfully strange author who admonished not to learn too much because all it produces is idle fantasies. After reading Samuel Johnson's *The Vanity of Human Wishes*, I had to ask myself if human life truly is a vicious, unhappy cycle. Because nature's gifts are conditional, when we achieve one thing do we lose another? Or put another way, the closer we get to something desired, do we desire it less because we now have it, and our reason for wanting it fades? Quintessential American thinker and nonconformist Ralph Waldo Emerson's emphasis on individualism, self-reliance, and the need to avoid conformity struck a chord in my psyche. I realized how much of my life had been lived in order to conform to others' opinions. Emerson wrote that we should live now and not in the past or future because time is passing, and with its passing, we miss opportunities. He thought that too many people fail to take the step from knowing to doing, and living is about doing. Mark Twain's irreverent snips at religion and admonitions to question authority in *Innocents Abroad* made me think about the many institutions and their rules back home that ruin lives. Voltaire's scathingly satiric response in *Candide* to Leibniz's view that this is the "best of all worlds" could quell the fervor of the most ardent optimist. It was humbling to read Voltaire's account of the many evils caused by man. I laughed at his account of work, which was that it keeps us from the three great evils: boredom, vice and poverty. Rabelais's wonderfully outrageous *Gargantua and Pantagruel* made me feel good about myself again as a human. He describes us as basically cheerful, good and perfect. His optimistic motto was "do what you will," which was precisely what I was doing.

I have always been attracted to philosophy because I believe it causes us to think deeper, universally, and from many perspectives. I like its search for truth. I have always found it comfortable to detach myself from reality and observe circumstances from a distance. Philosophy comes to me quite naturally. These qualities of philosophy are the reasons I had studied it at Whitman, Portland State University, and later in life at Oregon State University, where I obtained a master's degree in the subject. During my Aegean summer, I pursued this sense of philosophic detachment by reading over eighty excerpts from the best philosophic works ever written. I began with Confucius and Plato, and ended with Wittgenstein and Rawls. This made my intellectual escape also a deeply contemplative one.

Reading Plato's universal ideals caused me to think beyond existence. Kant made me consider the importance of duty in ethics and the nature of knowledge with his idealistic philosophy. Aristotle's doctrine of the mean caused me to consider the importance of temperance, and his virtue ethics, the role of virtue in happiness. With Diogenes the cynic I began to consider the insignificance of possessions and commonly held opinions. Reading Epictetus the stoic and Epicurus the epicurean made me consider their contrasting views for happiness—does happiness come from seeking pleasure or denying emotion? David Hume's idea that action does not arise from reason but rather from the sentiments confounded and challenged some of my deeply held beliefs. G. E. Moore's naturalistic fallacy was a challenge to answer: Are there some words, like "yellow," that cannot be further defined? Friedrich Nietzsche stood out in my readings because his overman, a hypothetically independent and willful individual, was relevant to my thinking. I needed a will to power to avoid living with false hopes and beliefs, to be skeptical of conventional morality and to find value beyond the accepted practices of my time in order to escape the life I had in a cube. If God is dead, I thought, then it is incumbent upon me to make the most of my life now.

Of all my readings in philosophy, I was most taken with the philosophy of the ancient stoics. In fact, I became a stoic. We use the word "stoic" today in a way that misrepresents the philosophy. Cicero, Seneca, Epictetus, and Marcus Aurelius were key Roman stoic philosophers who developed a philosophy of life that was intended to bring happiness to individuals. From these stoic masters, I learned to superintend my emotions because, when indulged, they can be a great source of unhappiness. I learned to remain indifferent to that which is beyond my choice, to live naturally and simply in accordance with nature, and to eschew opinion and convention. Studying philosophy, and particularly stoicism, caused a life-transforming alteration in my deeply held beliefs

in a way that dramatically improved my human condition. Later in life, I went on to obtain a master's degree in philosophy that focused on stoicism and the happiness it may bring others who face the same challenges in life I had before my Aegean summer.

    Greece was the right choice of a place to change my life. Being in a foreign culture with a strong intellectual heritage, people who live slower lives closer to nature, the warm and balmy climate and the water were circumstances conducive to change. I got a full measure of Greek culture on Ios by shopping in the local grocery, talking with old men in cafés, and getting to know a few individuals like Demetri and Georgias the local farmer. Being exposed to a culture so different from America's changed me. It is kind of like a small town's culture—everyone knows everyone else, the pace of life is slower, people live with the essentials of life and people seem to care. It was eye opening to be able to juxtapose my own culture with another because it gave me a new perspective and perhaps a better way of looking at things. Sure, the material rewards in America are great, but here were very happy Greek people living their simple lives without a lot of things. I always believed I did not need things to be happy, but in Greece I learned that this is not just a platitude, it is true. One lasting consequence of this revelation was my reluctance to acquire new things and zeal in discarding old things after the summer.

    With my family, I also expanded my Greek horizons by visiting, in addition to Athens, the Aegean islands of Mykonos, Naxos, and Santorini. I think our élan for life, our spirit of wanting to live, is heightened with adventure. Working in a cube in an American company breeds conformity and a need for security. This is a limited perspective because conformity debases our individuality and the desire for security undermines our aspirations for freedom. Adventure is the stuff of life; it brings newness, excitement, and a certain vitality to our lives. Perhaps it is the risk inherent in adventure that revitalizes our essential natures. In any case, it was not so much going to the Greek islands that was meaningful, but rather the adventurous process of just doing it. Mykonos is a commercialized tourist-oriented destination of interest, but the adventure was in getting there. We took a decrepit legendary ferry, the Ios Express to Mykonos, crowded with reveling holiday teenagers that rocked and rolled like a bathtub in the waves full of seasick people, including my wife. It was a grand adventure.

Our trip to the island of Naxos, which is just north of Ios, was uneventful. Naxos is a less touristy and more native Greek island. We stayed in a downtown hotel, walked the main cities streets and baked in the sun. Santorini is a jewel. It is a village clinging to the rim of an ancient underwater volcano. We spent most of the day there exploring and eating. We were so taken with the island that we missed the last ferry back to Ios and had to scramble to find a place to spend the night. In hindsight I think my forgetfulness and lack of attention was a good sign. Before, in business, I always had to be on top of everything. I had become a robot-like computer because my job demanded I know all the details, all the answers and what to do next. It was good to be a little forgetful and befuddled. Thankfully, it all worked out in the end. We found a place to spend the night and caught a ferry in the morning back to Ios. Ahh, it was a grand adventure.

On Ios, I took two significant excursions—Manganari bay and Klima. I was thinking about a complete change of lifestyle—one completely different from the one I left back home. I was thinking of a new home—a new existence. So, one day, I rented a motorcycle and drove to the extreme isolated southern end of the island and found a beautiful crescent shaped bay call Manganari. It was awesome. The sand was white and the water was crystal clear and warm. It was such an inviting Shangri-la. I pondered building a house on this bay and living there the rest of my life with my family. I was enthralled with the ideas of something new, of total relaxation, and of the happiness living in a beachfront villa. I was thrilled with the idea of escape and creating a new kind of existence. I was filled with desire to buy some land and build a villa.

My excitement was accentuated when one of the owners of our house invited us to visit them at a house they had built on a secluded nearby bay named Klima. It was an American enclave of three houses built overlooking a beautiful isolated white sandy beach and bay. I thought to myself that these people actually did build their dreams, and there was no reason I could not do likewise. My thoughts were spinning with dreams and the prospect of a new life.

This longing began something I had not expected—an honest and objective re-evaluation of my life back home. The more I thought about building at Manganari, the more I was flooded with contradictory thoughts. I was caught between desire and reality that precipitated considerable soul searching. I began to think about practical things like food, water, and sewage. I began to think of the consequences to my family, and in particular my children. How would they be educated and what would their lives be like growing up in isolation? I started thinking of the good things home in America had to offer—things I had always taken for granted. I thought of clean running water, abundance, culture, friends, and even the thrill of making money. It occurred to me how much I had only counted my problems back home, rarely my blessings. I never did pursue that dream house on Manganari bay and have always wondered what my life would be like today if I had.

Most Greeks are Orthodox Catholics, so it came as a real surprise to me to see many naked sunbathers on the beach. The island had become a kind of Mecca for young people seeking summer fun. It was not unusual to find a quarter of the beachgoers totally natural. The family would go to the beach and we would find ourselves amongst naked men and women of all ages. It really did not bother me, and I must admit many of the women looked pretty good. My first prudish American reaction was not to look at the women out of courtesy—I thought it was a matter of chivalry. But as time went on my attitude changed. I thought to myself "if these women fell free to be naked then it seems only right that I have the freedom to look." So I did. My wife warmed to the occasion faster than I and soon began going topless. My

My summer caused me to understand this family dynamic, and I began to appreciate the need to accentuate the good side of a family due to the incredible benefits it unleashes—in particular, happiness. Deep happiness comes from living within a group of people who love one another, like a family. I lived with three generations:—my mother and step-father, my wife, and my children—and I came to know the joys of companionship, closeness, warmth and support that lay latent within the family.

Children are a blessing and a curse. When my children were born, my life was permanently changed. I could no longer do what I pleased, I had to force myself to meet a higher standard, I was saddled with responsibility, I had to force myself to work to support them and I lost my freedom. I was resentful and unhappy—and it showed. My Aegean summer changed this perception. I was given a window of time to just be with my children and to enjoy them without the awareness of my obligations. We just interacted spontaneously and, well, just had fun. Things changed—I changed.

I suppose I changed because I began asking myself why I was drawn to my children. I began asking what their significance is. My answer was that we are born, we live and we die, and my question was, "Is that all there is?" If I had eschewed having children and lived a selfish life pursuing the gods of money, security, prestige, power or sensual pleasure, what would I have that is worthwhile in life? What would my life be like when I was sixty? It occurred to me that all I would have had is just more of the same, nothing would have changed, and I would die a forgettable worthless human knowing that I had

added little to humanity. Children seem to change this equation—they are part of us, they come from us and they perpetuate us. They are that eminently meaningful link in the chain of our human experience. To have them, to get to know them, to fashion them in your image and to love them is the real stuff of life. I was fortunate to learn this valuable lesson during my Aegean summer. I came to appreciate my children, love them, and get closer to them, and this lesson served me well throughout the rest of my life.

I spent my summer just playing with my young children. We swam, we ran, we swam, we explored, we swam, we ate together and then we swam some more. It was like being a kid again and having some really neat related playmates.

My role as father to young children has now faded, and my children have forgotten many of the summer things we did together. In many ways, parenting is a thankless job—our children move on to other lives and away from us. They never know the sacrifices their parents made. But the point of parenting is not about us but rather them, and if we are good parents, they leave us and become independent. This is the paradox of parenting—we raise our children to leave us. My journey with my young children went by like a flash, but I had the rare opportunity to capture a precious moment in time with them on Ios.

So many of our mental and physical maladies come from living in demanding, pressure-filled, artificial environments such as those found in the American workplace. America is a society of commerce. It values productivity, money, aggression, competitiveness, status and power. It has little room for the individual and the individual's desires and needs. We become like rats in a maze. The maze was designed by the society, and we are expected to navigate its corridors. Our lives become one of obligation and duty. We succumb to forging links to the chain our forefathers created. We lose touch with what we want and what we need as individuals. Many of our diseases are a consequence of this artificial environment. Heart disease, alcoholism, anxiety, depression and ulcers are largely culturally created. I escaped those circumstances and was living a natural life. Nature truly is easily satisfied. Focus on the simple things to live a long and happy life—don't make things complicated.

Bertrand Russell believed that when we focus excessively on work, we lose our perspective on life. The result is fatigue, nervous strain and the inability to be interested in matters unrelated to work. The ultimate consequence is unhappiness. I believe our American work ethic fosters this myopic mindset with its emphasis on work and success. We become so absorbed in our own small pursuits that we lose our perspectives on life. Life is expansive; it should be full, and it should include a variety of activities and interests to be healthy and balanced. It is amazing how much there is—so much to think and so much to do in this world.

Without an expansive view of the world, Russell believed that we come to overstate our own importance. We become petty, self-seeking individuals who are troubled by trivial misfortunes, dreading what fate may have in store for us. My solution was to turn away from the world of commerce and explore what alternatives the world had to offer. In doing so, I found that the angst and anxiety that I had acquired over time abated. I found, as Russell pointed out, that fear of the future, fear of falling behind my competitors, and even the fear of death, faded. What I learned was that the person who can forget his or her work, even for a short time, is better off than the one who continually worries about it.

As time passed, my body and mind became grounded, and I began living within the cycle of nature and not opposed to it. I became more tranquil. I just got happy. Life was pleasant. My angst melted. I could not wait to live. Something had happened to me. When I was not influenced by outside forces, I came to learn more about myself. When the artificiality of my life was shed, I naturally got closer to my true nature. I came to hear the inner voice that had been muted by layers and layers of hype and propaganda. This voice talked to me, I listened, and my self emerged like a photograph being developed. It was an easy process, and who I was became clear. I learned that I enjoyed business, the city and the challenges of my profession of commercial real estate. I enjoyed the thrill of making money. I liked people; I enjoyed my friends and extended family—and missed them. I liked the hustle, bustle and excitement of commerce. I actually missed what was going on back home.

My wife and I had long talks about our future. We debated whether we should stay or go home. We were both prepared to go either way. As time passed and we explored our feelings, lives and future in-depth, the decision became increasingly clear. We decided that our future lay with where we were born, grew up and started our family home. So we left Ios for home in late August 1992. My Aegean summer had come to an end.

On the return from Greece, we made a side trip to Cairo, Egypt. There we walked along the Nile, saw the pyramids at Giza, the Sphinx, the Egyptian National Museum, the Sultan Hasan Mosque and the old bazaar. It was a wonderful adventure with my family. We had coffee in an Egyptian coffee house similar to the one described in Naguib Mahfouz's books, ate lunch in the famous Groppi's restaurant, and watched the dhows float on the Nile from our hotel veranda in the evening. From Cairo we flew to Athens, London, and then home.

In addition to growing a beard and long hair, my summer made me a new man. I had changed. I gained a broader philosophic and optimistic perspective on living. The feeling of oppression and responsibility were gone, and my demons went looking for other victims. My anxieties, troubles and worries had disappeared. I looked forward to living. I was interested in the future—I was interested in everything. I had much more to think about, and I did much more thinking. I was happy.

CHAPTER THREE

AFTER THE SUMMER

I returned to Portland in the fall of 1992 in high spirits—everything seemed new and fresh. Nothing had really changed. The airport, freeways, neighborhoods and people were pretty much as I had left them. What changed was me. I saw everything through new eyes. The webs of oppressive ideas, the weight of ideologies and the heavy, entangling obligations had all dissipated. Gone was the ever-present feeling of competition and fear of falling behind. Gone was the myriad of desires that had plagued my psyche and equanimity. The world did not feel like a hostile place—it was an oyster. My attitude, or perhaps perception of these kinds of life problems, had changed. They seemed more like fun challenges rather than obstacles to overcome. I did not feel fear or dread. I was concerned, but I felt good—both mentally and physically. I felt strong and healthy and was eager to tackle any obstacle life had to offer. I felt totally alive, interested, and anxious to reexamine what I had left. It was good to be home.

Certainly, there were many challenges to reassimilating into society on my terms. The first was money. I had a little savings to live on as well as some of the proceeds of the sale of my house to buy a new house. Money was tight, but I was confident that once I got back to work, money would take care of itself. I think that the loss of money, or the fear of being without money, is the greatest deterrent to people considering changing their lives. I think this is a healthy attitude, but that it is too often blown out of proportion. I lost some money, but it was small in relation to my overall assets. More importantly, what is your happiness worth? Is it worth it to spend some of your assets in order to revitalize your life and rekindle élan for living? The experience is worth far more than a bigger number in an account. What I found was that when I returned to work, money did take care of itself.

My second problem was to find a place for us to live. We first rented a cramped apartment for a few months while looking for a new house. Fortune was kind—the builder of our last house had, unbeknownst to me, taken all of our suggestions on how to improve it and built a new house while we were gone. When we first saw the new house we could not believe it because it had everything we wanted. It was in a quiet, close-in neighborhood on a private lane. It had all the room for my family and a large yard for my children. We immediately bought it and moved in just in time to enjoy Thanksgiving in our new home. It was a thrill retrieving our furniture from the mini-storage facility and arranging the house just the way we wanted.

My third problem was to revitalize my commercial real estate practice. I returned to my old employer, which was a surreal experience. It was not so much me but the environment that was unreal. Many of the sources of my past unhappiness quickly returned. The workplace environment was the same. It was a place of serious people in an artificial hurry to make more money before they die and give it all to someone else. It was still a place of intense competition and the pressure to produce. I told myself that I could just not live in this kind of environment again—it was oppressive and utterly unnecessary. I did not need this kind of environment to support my family or live. What I really did not like was the old life in a cube, being a cog in a machine and a transparent individual. I quickly felt trapped just like I had felt when I left—the same old feelings of repression and resentment began anew. But things were now different—I had changed because I had experienced freedom, which made the work environment intolerable. I just thought to myself,

"This will not work." I had experienced freedom, and I had learned not to fear change, so I took a deep breath and quit.

 I had always wanted to own my own business, so I started my own company, John L. Bowman, Realtor. It was scary. I had no listings, I had to find a place to work, and I was without structure for the first time in my work career. This was something I had always wanted to do but never got up the courage to act. But my Aegean summer had taught me that change is often good and that most anything is possible if I just try. I was lucky, my practice began with a bang—I got some great listings and made some large lease transactions right off the bat. I think some of my success was due to my experience in the business, but I also think some people were vicariously rooting for me and secretly helping my nascent company succeed. It was amazing because so many things started working in my favor. I started making twice the money because I did not have to share my commissions with a company, and I worked with half the stress because the environment was not competitive. To top it all, I was a free individual setting my own agendas, goals, and schedules. After starting my own practice, I was reminded of how much I enjoyed being a man of commerce where money changes hands, negotiations are often high stake and, above all, where I could earn lots of money. It was fun and exciting—I was glad to be back.

 I was reminded of two things I had read over the summer: that the wind works for the man with a goal and fortune favors the brave. When you have a goal, circumstances conspire to help you achieve it. You spot opportunities, many people help when they know what you want and a goal energizes you. Goals exude an infectious, positive and optimistic attitude that just breeds success. Fortune favors the brave because fortune likes brave people. The risk and inevitable failures the brave incur are more than offset by the rewards reaped by those who have the courage to try new things. At a minimum, if you never try you will never succeed. Stasis, conventionality, status quo and fear are cul-de-sacs.

Starting my new business is an example. I found that fortune militated in my favor because I had a goal and the courage to act. I had the goal so I worked harder, I was more optimistic, my clients wanted me to succeed, I wanted to succeed and I got more exposure because it was now my name on the sign—which in turn brought more business. None of these would have happened if I had not taken the risk. And if I lacked courage I would never have had the opportunity to succeed at all. Certainly, I could have failed, but with courage I would keep trying until I did succeed. Fortune was on my side.

We all face times in our lives where we must make a decision to do something where the consequences are unknown. But we can never make the perfect decision because we never have all the information to make the perfect decision. There will always be unknown variables. So, the decisions we make to change our lives are really educated guesses that require a leap of faith—a leap that involves our intuition. But many do not take that leap because they do not trust their intuition. They have allowed fear to override their intuition because they fear the unknown—or as Shakespeare put it, they prefer to live unhappily with the problems they know than the problems they know not. I think one key to happiness is the ability to trust our intuitions, engage our will, summon our courage and act in order to do what we really want to do in life.

My fourth problem was the most daunting. It was whether I could maintain the happiness I had achieved during my summer within a culture that had made me so unhappy. How could I realign my new beliefs and attitudes with American culture in order to be happy? In order to succeed again in my profession, I was quickly faced with the need to resurrect my competitive spirit and former aggressive nature. The problem was that I had become more pensive and less competitive. I had lived in a different, slower culture with different values, and I had come to appreciate what a relaxed culture has to offer. It was a dilemma—on one hand I enjoyed my work, but on the other I found the excessive go-go hustle and bustle, commercialism and drive found in American culture wearisome. This was my greatest challenge: How to re-acculturate in such a way that would preserve my happiness.

My solution was to negotiate a balance. I retained my appreciation for American culture and what it has to offer. Like my life before the summer, I worked hard, pursued deals and competed with other brokers. But, due to my Aegean summer, I was more able to keep it all in perspective. I unwittingly adopted a more come-what-may, insouciant and relaxed attitude. I came to view work as one small component of life that is necessary, but not the most important—more as an interesting challenge than an end in itself. I began to take more days off and do something else like take naps in the afternoon. I found that this detachment took the fearfulness out of work, and the result was that I actually enjoyed work more.

I also found that my attitudes, indeed my entire life philosophy toward life, changed. I saw marriage as a partnership with a lover and friend, children as my progeny, art and literature as fantastic, relationships as special, sports as exciting and challenging, health as special, and virtue as noble. Gone were the negative thoughts about obligations, limitations, competition and excessive ambition. These were just changes of perception, or simply different ways of looking at things that brought me a happier outlook on life. Certainly, the reasons for my past negative views still existed, but the reasons to look at things negatively had disappeared—they just no longer occurred to me.

Wendy Lustbader wrote a book titled *What's Worth Knowing* in which she endeavored to discern some of life's most important lessons. She did this by interviewing old people—people who had lived long lives. She asked them questions like, "How would you live your life differently knowing what you know now?" "What advice would you give young people just starting out in life?" And, "What are the keys to living a happy life?" They gave five recurring answers that I found most poignant: the first was to appreciate freedom; the second was to not worry about things that do not really matter; third, happiness does not come from buying things; fourth was to not fight things you cannot change; and finally, to accept each day for what it offers. At age forty-two, I was just learning these important lessons for a happy life.

To me, freedom means not only political freedom but also freedom of the mind. It means the ability to escape convention, to be able to put in perspective others' and society's demands, and the freedom to just think and act differently. On one level, I had the bills I had to pay, the clothes I had to wear, the taxes I had to pay and the car I had to maintain so I could get to work. My life was a checklist of what I must do in order to function in society. On another more sinister level, my success in life was determined by societal conventions—where I lived, how big my house was, who I knew and how much money I made. These are artificial criteria created by other people that I learned have nothing to do with who I am or my happiness. I came to realize that I could live a simple life outside of these oppressive conventions. My Aegean summer allowed me to escape these confining demands of American society and seek alternate possibilities in life. I gained the freedom to think differently. This is a priceless mental freedom that brought me happiness.

I learned that I spent a good deal of my life worrying excessively about unimportant matters. It seemed like there were so many important things to do that had to get done. I had to work between certain clock times, I had to make sure my daughter fed the dog and I had to make sure all the bills were paid on time. When I went to Greece, nothing had to get done (other than take a daily swim). We create for ourselves a virtual world of pressing obligations and then fret over them. I found that I had blown small issues all out of proportion. Sure, the lawn needs mowing and the roof needs reshingling, but these are not issues that ought to drive my life or determine my happiness. I had been spending my life worrying about things that caused me unhappiness, but in the big picture they really did not matter.

One significant, unimportant worry I learned to shed is what people think of me. Many of us unwittingly are very concerned what others think of us, and in particular whether we are liked. Many spend considerable effort shielding their true selves in order to be liked. The truth is that we should just accept the fact that some will not like us and live life accepting this. We should not fear what others think. I learned this because I spent time away from my contemporaries' judging gaze, and I learned what they thought ultimately was irrelevant to my happiness. I learned that I should just relax, be myself and let the chips fall where they may.

Lustbader's elderly people consistently said that they had learned in life that happiness does not come from owning things. Perhaps the pride of ownership comes from our instinct to survive—if our ancestors owned a good hut and ox they were happy because they were better able to live. This sounds intuitively right. But today our good hut becomes a bigger house with rooms we do not need, and our ox becomes a Land Rover with four-wheel drive that we never use. I was once gripped with the desire for a grand house. It was awesome—a large colonial house with a pool and expansive lawn. I was gripped with a passion to own this mansion that was insatiable. But my Aegean summer caused me to ask why owning this house was so important. I said to myself that I did not need it, I did not need to impress my friends, and I really did not need the debt I would have to incur to buy it. I realized that owning my imaginary house had nothing to do with what really made me happy. I learned to be satisfied with little and forgot the house.

If you think about it, we are a lot like a dog on a leash. The dog has some freedom within the length of the leash and none beyond it. There are some things we have some control over in life, like who our friends are, who we marry and when we go to bed. But like the dog's tether, God has limited our choices in life. We have no control over whether we die or get struck by lightning—matters that cause many people to worry and fret. But why? Why worry about that which you cannot control? It is going to happen whether you worry or not, so why bother? The truth is we are happier people when we do not live in fear of fate—we should just accept fated matters and move on. I learned later in life that this is an old thought; it is one tenet of the ancient philosophic school of stoicism. Stoicism is a philosophy that endeavors to bring people happiness, and one way is to remain indifferent to that which you cannot control. The famous stoic Cicero, for example, was only consoled after the death of his daughter by telling himself there is nothing he can do to change it—continuous mourning only brought him unhappiness. I learned during my summer that I had wasted far too much time in life fretting over matters I could not change.

When I learned not to fight things, I also learned to accept each day for what it offers. It was like learning to stop struggling with shadows and beginning to accept things for what they really are, which is an attitude that inclined me to happiness. With this insight I began to be more grateful for what I had and not what I did not have, to appreciate what was occurring now, and to be less concerned with what bad things might happen in the future. I realized that much of my life had been lived trying to engineer outcomes. I had wanted to get people to do things that I wanted. I wanted my clients, wife and children to act in ways that I thought were the right ways. I was trying to engineer perfection, but perfection does not exist. What was missing from this equation was what made me happy. Because I was constantly trying to engineer my life and control others, I had set myself up for misery because people resist being controlled and fate is its own engineer. I learned that this was a dead-end street because the consequences were always frustration, disappointment and anger. I asked, "Why do this to myself?"

Certainly, we should have goals, and we should work toward those goals. They help us succeed in life. But sometimes those goals can become our prisons. We come to think we must do that, we must be this way, or we must achieve something. The truth is life is uncertain, and we should remain flexible in our attitudes and beliefs. This thought enables me to accept each day for what it offers and tack with the wind rather than fight it.

Many years after my summer I read *The Progress Paradox: How Life Gets Better While People Feel Worse* by Gregg Easterbrook, which gave me a significant insight why my experience in Greece had brought me so much happiness. I think I experienced a paradigmatic process that began with desire, required courage and ended with gratitude.

Like Plato, Easterbrook explained that a significant source of my unhappiness came from my desires. I wanted many things that I did not have, and it was the gap between having and wanting that was the essence of my unhappiness. I wanted what everyone wants, things like freedom, security, wealth and love. In my case, it was mostly freedom and security. I wanted freedom from my life obligations and the security to live as I wanted to live. I was constantly thinking that my life could be better, and it was this feeling that caused most of my negative, unhappy feelings.

I particularly desired materialistic security. What I learned was that I had over-emphasized this desire—it had come to control far too much of my life. I was forever judging my well being not by where I stood, but rather by whether I thought my material circumstances would improve. I lived in fear that the future would bring me less. I was dreaming of unnecessary and uncertain future benefits while at the same time fearing the loss of what I had. I feared losing my standard of living and the relative freedom it provided me. In real terms I feared losing my home, job and money. I feared the loss of security, but that fear was robbing my freedom.

The solution did not come easily; it was to summon my courage in order to mitigate my desires. It takes courage to staunch desire. Like many, I was stuck in a comfortable, depressing rut, unwilling to change my life. I preferred to live with the problems I knew. Every time I wanted to escape my obligations, I would always return to my rut of comfort and security. I would always end up asking myself, "What will I do and how will I survive if I leave my job?" I also suffered from self-doubt because I feared making the wrong decisions. Courage can be difficult to summon, but the thought that my life was half over and that if I did not act now the rest of it would just be more of the same emboldened me to act.

Once I acted, things changed. I found myself living slower in a totally different environment, which enabled me to put my desires, indeed my whole life, in perspective.

From this new perspective, I learned many things, including appreciating what I had. I found that this newly learned sense of gratitude diminished my pangs of desire because I came to realize how really good my life was. Gratitude was the antidote for my paradigm of unhappiness. Before my summer I rarely felt contented because I was always concerned about something, anticipating problems, or just anxious. I was always thinking about what was wrong with things and not what was right. In the big picture, my life was great, but I could not see through the fog of desire. Courage gave me the chance to clear that fog so I could see how easy it is to live simply without the need for more. I was reminded of Thoreau's admonition to simplify life, and the cynic Diogenes's comment that a man's happiness is measured by what he does not want.

I think Easterbrook described a paradigmatic way of thinking that American culture accentuates that causes many unhappiness. It is a paradigm that I was caught in before I went to Greece, it is the paradigm I escaped from for a period of time and it is a paradigm that I did not want to return to. This paradigm blinded me to my alternatives and sapped my will to change my circumstances. It was not only my lack of courage, but also ignorance of my ontological freedom. The result was emptiness and lack of meaning in my life. I was stuck in a rut, unable to envision other ways of living and thinking. It was only through the courage to change and resulting appreciation for what I had gained during my Aegean summer that I came to understand and discard this paradigm that had brought me so much unhappiness.

One unexpected consequence of my Aegean summer was other people's reactions. A few were critical. They accused me of abandoning my career, putting my family in jeopardy or just being irresponsible. Some even called me eccentric, which I take as a compliment if eccentricity entails the pursuit of happiness. These were the exceptions; the vast majority reacted with joy, wonder and the desire to do the same thing. It seemed everyone wanted to know what I did, how I did it and particularly how I changed. People wanted to hear a happy story that they themselves might live.

Most were working people like me in jobs they chaffed at, and they all yearned for something new. Like me, they wanted more from life. I was amazed how they would hang on every word as I described my experience as if the life I was describing could happen to them.

At first people would be excited, energized and almost exuberant. They all would say that they would like to do the same thing. But then reality would always settle in and they would get serious, begin to express worries and start explaining all the reasons why they could not do what I did. They would say that they did not have the money, they could not leave their job, or they had too many obligations. But these were precisely the same obstacles I faced before my Aegean summer. I came to think of them as a bird in a cage with an open door. They were free to take that door and fly to freedom, but the comfort of the cage and familiarity of the bars was their psychic comfort zone. For some strange reason, it made them feel good to live trapped. I think they feared newness, challenge or the unknown—which is certainly understandable. But they were like birds in a cage pondering that open door, unwilling to fly to freedom because they did not know what was outside the door. They, like the bird, were free but not free because they were the prisoners of their own thoughts.

Some summoned the courage and flew the coop. One courageous colleague was so taken by my story he quit his firm and started his own company. Another, George Macoubray, who is mentioned in the introduction to this book, immediately made arrangements to take his wife and family on a three-month trip of Europe. Some people reacted with enthusiasm and others with a kneejerk fear of the unknown; some thought they would and others thought they could not; some mustered the courage and others showed fear. I could not help but think to myself how much the latter were locked in their self-made mental cages living pedestrian, anxious lives just doing more of the same. If you desire happiness, think freedom and take the chance.

After my Aegean summer my life changed for the better. I took things more philosophically. I became more detached. I watched life from afar. I sent all of my suits to the cleaners and then neatly put them in the closet where they sit to this day. My hairstyle unconsciously changed from a part down one side, which represented conformity, to straight back, which symbolized freedom and individualism. I stopped setting the dreaded alarm clock in the morning and began waking up naturally. Surprisingly, I found myself going to bed earlier, drinking less, and getting up earlier feeling great. Perhaps most significantly my attitudes changed dramatically. Money and possessions became less important, and I valued time more. What I owned became less important than what I experienced. Desires no longer ruled my life. I felt less repressed, and I felt in control of my own destiny.

To my surprise I came to enjoy people more. I came to realize how much I had objectified people. I had considered them obligations, enemies, competitors, sources of money or just a bother. People had irritated me. But I had changed. I lost this misanthropic edge to my worldview and now found people interesting. I saw them more as companions taking this very short and strange journey of life with me, facing and struggling with the same problems and obstacles.

I learned that if you look and listen hard and long enough, there is always something unique or interesting about someone. Even people's faults interested me. The dull and prideful, particularly the prideful, offered some interesting lessons. I observed arrogant people who thought they were better than others—special—and the result was always the same: pride goeth before the fall. I came to observe a certain timeless pattern of human characteristics and their inevitable consequences. Overly sensuous people committed adultery and divorced, avaricious people were greedy and cold and those who sought prestige were forever jealous of competitors. I came to realize that the ancient philosophers were right; virtue is indeed needed to be happy. With virtue, we mitigate these unnecessary desires and the pejorative consequences they bring.

I also found out about judgment during my summer. Before my summer I was judgmental—especially of people. To be judgmental is not necessarily bad because good judgment tells us that, for example, we ought not hire an accountant who can't add. But I think competitive societies like America accentuate our inclination to judge, and the consequence is we miss opportunities to know other kinds of people; people who are worthy in their own way. I cut people off. I came to realize how many opportunities to meet interesting, different and thoughtful people I had lost due to my judgmental nature. In my former hustle-bustle life, I was too busy judging to take the time to simply listen and talk. Someone would call or I would bump into an acquaintance on the street, but I was always too busy. After my summer I found myself slowing down and accepting people more for what they are—I took the time to listen. I found life far more interesting and rewarding when I stopped judging and began to reconnect with people on a human level. It all just made for a better life for me.

My personality changed. I began to see more humor in most everything. I began to laugh at the human condition, the irony in supercilious behavior and most of all the humor in people. People can be funny if you just look and listen hard enough. People like humor, and they repay humor with humor when possible. It is infectious. Just a little humor takes the edge off of life's problems, facilitates human relations and is a powerful antidote to worry and depression. It truly is God's gift to man and a major source of happiness.

My attitude toward work completely changed. Many of the sources of my unhappiness evaporated when I started my own company. I dressed relaxed, my time was my own and, above all, I was no longer trapped in an artificial dog-eat-dog environment. I took great pride in being the owner of my own business. I felt liberated because I was independent and in control of my own destiny. I was still competitive, but I now kept it in perspective. I won a few and lost a few, and I felt grateful that I won sometimes. The result of this was amazing—I found myself working more and enjoying doing business. I also found myself making twice the money with half the stress.

Other facets of my life changed: I spent more time with my friends and family, I played more of my favorite sport volleyball, I spent more time working on small things and relaxing in my yard and I read much more. My entire outlook on life was different. I began to take a much bigger view of life and to appreciate how precious and incredibly short it is. I became calmer and more tranquil. I developed a lighter and happier personality that was positive and optimistic rather than dour—my demeanor changed. I felt free, and I was happy.

CHAPTER FOUR

CONCLUSION

Sophocles once said that man too often waits to the evening to see how splendid the day has been. We have only one life to live, and it is a mistake not to live it. We spend the best part of our young lives shouldering obligations, like making money, in order to enjoy a questionable liberty during the last and least valuable part of it. We give our lives away to obligations and responsibility. We will all die soon and be forgotten, so what we do here and now is all that is important. We view time as a measurable unit that is spent; we do not think in terms of passing time. We squander our limited time alive busily forging those endless links to the chain that ultimately connects nothing. We live our lives indebted to dead people, when in reality the world is for the living. Society represses us with duty and punishes us if we fail to conform. Our individuality becomes subordinated to the group. We come to live in the opinion of others, and their judgments become our prisons.

The goal of life is not death. Death is inevitable, so accept it and make the most of life while we can. There is a difference between accepting death and resigning ourselves to it with the attitude that nothing matters. Do not wait to die. We were not born to sit in God's waiting room impotently anticipating the end. Life is too short, precious, wonderful, exuberant and exciting to be wasted in a resigned and defeated state of mind.

Look at the photograph of me taken during my summer of 1992 on Ios in the azure Aegean Sea with my children. This picture shows what is perhaps the happiest time of my life. Maude is about eight, Abbey six and Sydney three. I was studying literature and philosophy, I was relaxed, my family surrounded me, I was enjoying incredible sex with my beautiful wife and I was physically fit. I was sleeping long and deeply, I swam every day, I was reading, I was running, I had evening dinners with my family and I was spending dusk sitting on a roof veranda drinking Metaxa 5 Star Brandy watching the sun set with Curt talking about ideas. All of my physical and emotional needs were totally satisfied. The sun was bright, the evenings were cool and clear, the water was tropical, and life was good. I had lost the knot in my stomach, and I felt no angst. I was supremely happy. I think anyone with the will to change can achieve what I did in this photo.

I was happy because my Aegean summer taught me two important lessons in life: I learned not to waste my time on unnecessary and self-defeating desires, and I learned that things are as we make them.

Boethius wrote that we submit to fortune because we desire things like wealth, position, power, fame and sensual pleasure. We think if we could only achieve these desired ends, we will win happiness, but what we find is that we don't for many reasons. We find that we forever want something we do not have or have enough of. We are always wanting to change our condition. Our desires just engender more desires, and these ends constantly fluctuate as well as our successes in achieving them. If we do by chance achieve one of these ends, we live in constant fear of losing what we have gained, and we are fraught with anxiety because nothing is constant. For Boethius, the crux of our unhappiness—even bitterness—occurs when fortune thwarts our desires.

Seneca believed that peace and contentment do not come when high values are set on externals because they can be taken away. Externals are all those things that are beyond our control like wealth, position, power, fame, and sensual pleasure—the same list as Boethius's. Seneca never trusted fortune because nobody has ever been "crushed by adverse Fortune who has not first been beguiled by her smile" (Hadas 112).

They spoke, and I learned. I unwittingly had imagined a certain way of living that caused me to think that I had to have a certain level of material wealth in order to be happy. What I did not consider was that my imagination was creating a standard that I really did not need, and it was this standard that drove my desire for money. I learned in Greece that materialistic American culture drives this imaginary standard. I had little during my summer, and I was supremely happy. I learned the importance of living a simple life.

I had never pondered how much wealth I truly needed. Boethius said that riches create a want of their own, and once they are won they never leave us free. Money never satisfies. I was on a treadmill, always thinking I needed more money to be happy. I was always measuring my happiness in relation to someone who had money, but when I made money I was never satisfied because I always thought I needed more money. I learned that I was caught in a self-defeating belief when in reality nature is easily satisfied.

I was so caught up in the pursuit of money that I failed to consider that there are better ends than money and enduring sources of happiness. Money is a man-created thing that can be alienated, but the sight of a beautiful countryside, a woman's smile, a friend's pat on the back, or our children's innocent embrace are more profound. These experiences come easily, whereas money is hard and unemotional. I learned to realign my values and focus on truer sources of happiness.

Because I was so preoccupied with wealth and security, I also failed to appreciate the consequences of my desires. It was my desires that forced me to endure the circumstances that caused my unhappiness. I lived under a delusion thinking that the artificial and competitive office environment was natural. I learned that my desire for security had driven me to live in a world I despised—a world that was not what I needed or really wanted.

The second thing I learned was that my happiness is within my control. Happiness is not something to find, but rather something to create. I think it was Shakespeare, Boethius and Seneca that convinced me of this.

Shakespeare wrote that there is nothing either good or bad, but thinking makes it so; Boethius wrote nothing is miserable unless we think it so; and Seneca wrote the world is as we make it. These three authors, who spanned two-thousand years of human history, were describing the same timeless source of unhappiness—the mind. They were also describing the same timeless way to happiness—again, the mind. Reading these philosophers changed my mind, and the result was that I became happier. They all described happiness as the consequence of our mental attitudes—attitudes that shape and form our worlds. The world truly is as we make it, and if we want to be happy, we need to look to ourselves and shape our minds to make it so.

For Boethius, true happiness is a condition of self-sufficiency with no wants. We are born naked, and we should not wear ourselves out by setting our hearts on wearing fancy clothes. We should live serene lives and smile at the raging storm. True happiness is that which makes us self-sufficient, strong, worthy of respect, glorious and joyful.

Seneca believed that things are what we make them—that it is our state of mind and attitude that determines much of our condition in life. For him, happiness lies within choice. There are some things that cause us unhappiness that we simply have no control over, so rather than allow them to cause us unhappiness, we should remain indifferent to them. It is the exigencies of fortune that we have no control over that become our masters. Epictetus wrote that the path to freedom is not to destroy the tyrant outside but rather the one within; to achieve happiness we must "turn out the tyrants within ourselves," which are those desires for things that are not within our ability to control (Epictetus 235).

I have often wondered what it would be like to live three-hundred years. If I could it would seem I could satisfy all of my desires. With the accumulation of knowledge and experience through time, I would be able to acquire unrivaled wealth, position, power, fame and sensual pleasure. A few dollars invested today would be worth millions in the future, endlessly currying favors would bring tremendous prestige, work would come easily as my competitors died off, just being known for a long time would bring fame and I would have three-hundred years to satisfy all my sensual desires. Every nook and cranny, every aspect, every one of my desires could be satisfied beyond imagination. But would I be happy?

I do not think so. Boethius and Seneca taught me that satisfying my desires does not necessarily bring happiness. More is at stake. If I lived three-hundred years, my parents would be dead, all of my childhood friends would be gone, my wife and children would be dead, all of the friends and acquaintances I acquired during my life would have died long ago, and even my grandchildren and great-grandchildren who I would come to know would be dead. My time would have passed, and I would be living like an alien in a strange world. I would be lost and unknown in a time not of my own. I do not think an immortality that satisfied all of my desires would bring me happiness. The greatest happiness is to be had now while I am alive with those I grew up with, the person I married, the children I procreated and the friends I made along the way. I learned that it is a tragedy not to appreciate this truth. I learned that we must live life now, appreciate what we have and mitigate our desires in order to be truly happy.

People ask me about my Aegean summer. They usually say that they wish they could do the same thing. They also want to escape their dreary lives with travel and adventure. Very few do. The reason is because they fear the unknown—they fear uncertainty. They would rather remain unhappily secure in the rut they know than face unknown circumstances. They fear trying something new because their lives might get worse. This is a self-defeating way of thinking that only perpetuates unhappiness. Certainly, things could get worse, but they might get better and they will never get better if you don't try. It is better to follow your heart in order to find a better and happier future. Even if a change does not work out, I figured I could always change again, and again and again until I got it right. Changing my life did not have to be a permanent, fixed-in-time solution, but rather an evolving process—an evolving solution. This dynamic and optimistic philosophy of life enabled me to find happiness.

The truth is that we will never live fully unless we take a chance. Our happiness literally depends on our resolve to change our lives. We must break out and learn to live our own lives as individuals pursuing our own dreams. We must have the courage to live life on our terms. It has been said that the greatest regret people have before they die is not doing in life what they really wanted to do in life. You must do what you want now before it is too late.

The summer of 1992 taught me these lessons, fulfilled my dreams and changed my life. It was the beginning of my liberation, which has continued unabated to this day. On my deathbed, I will consider it one of the most important things I did in my lifetime.

WORKS CITED

Duff, J. Wright. *The Literary History of Rome*. New York: Barnes and Noble, Inc., 1960.

Easterbrook, Gregg. *The Progress Paradox: How Life Gets Better While People Feel Worse*. New York: Random House, 2004.

Epictetus. *The Discourses*. London: Orion Publishing Group, 1995.

Freud, Sigmund. *Civilization and its Discontent*. New York: W. W. Norton & Co., 1961.

Hadas, Moses. *The Essential Works of Stoicism*. New York: Bantam Books, 1961.

Seneca. *The Stoic Philosophy of Seneca*. New York: W. W. Norton & Company, 1958.

James, William. *The Varieties of Religious Experience*. New York: Dover Publication, 2002.

Kirsch, M. M. *How to Get Off the Fast Track and Live a Life Money Can't Buy.* Los Angeles: Lowell House, 1991.

Lustbader, Wendy. *What's Worth Knowing*. New York: Penguin Group: 2004.

Mack, Maynard, General Editor. *Norton Anthology of World Masterpieces,* The New York: W. W. Norton, 1992.

Magill, Frank N, ed. *Masterpieces of World Philosophy*. New York: HarperCollins Publishers, 1990.

Nussbaum, Martha C. *The Therapy of Desire: Theory and Practice in Hellenistic Ethics*. Princeton: Princeton University Press, 1994.

Rifkin, Jeremy. *Time Wars; The Primary Conflict of Human History*. New York: Henry Holt and Company, 1987.

Russell, Bertrand. *The Conquest of Happiness*. New York: Avon Books, 1930 copyright.

The map in chapter two is from "Welcome to the Greek Islands," at http://www.greek-islands.us/. Accessed June 3, 2010.

www.ingramcontent.com/pod-product-compliance
Lightning Source LLC
Chambersburg PA
CBHW060530010526
44110CB00052B/2550